VELOCIRAPTOR

by Arnold Ringstad

Cody Koala
An Imprint of Pop!
popbooksonline.com

abdobooks.com
Published by Pop!, a division of ABDO, PO Box 398166, Minneapolis, Minnesota 55439. Copyright © 2019 by POP, LLC. International copyrights reserved in all countries. No part of this book may be reproduced in any form without written permission from the publisher. Pop!™ is a trademark and logo of POP, LLC.

Printed in the United States of America, North Mankato, Minnesota.

082018
012019

THIS BOOK CONTAINS RECYCLED MATERIALS

Cover Photo: iStockphoto
Interior Photos: iStockphoto, 1, 10, 13; Chris Butler/Science Source, 5; Shutterstock Images, 6, 15, 16, 19; Millard H. Sharp/Science Source, 7, 9 (top), 9 (bottom right); Dirk Wiersma/Science Source, 9 (bottom left); Francois Gohier/Science Source, 20

Editor: Meg Gaertner
Series Designer: Laura Mitchell

Library of Congress Control Number: 2018949757
Publisher's Cataloging-in-Publication Data
Names: Ringstad, Arnold, author.
Title: Velociraptor / by Arnold Ringstad.
Description: Minneapolis, Minnesota : Pop!, 2019 | Series: Dinosaurs | Includes online resources and index.
Identifiers: ISBN 9781532161841 (lib. bdg.) | ISBN 9781641855556 (pbk) | ISBN 9781532162909 (ebook)
Subjects: LCSH: Velociraptor--Juvenile literature. | Dinosaurs--Juvenile literature. | Extinct animals--Juvenile literature.
Classification: DDC 567.912--dc23

Hello! My name is

Cody Koala

Pop open this book and you'll find QR codes like this one, loaded with information, so you can learn even more!

Scan this code* and others like it while you read, or visit the website below to make this book pop.

popbooksonline.com/velociraptor

*Scanning QR codes requires a web-enabled smart device with a QR code reader app and a camera.

Table of Contents

Chapter 1

A Swift Thief

Velociraptor was a small **predator**. It ran on two legs. It had sharp teeth and claws. Its name means "swift thief."

Watch a video here!

Velociraptor was
about the size of a turkey.
It likely hunted small reptiles
and dinosaurs.

It lived during the
Cretaceous Period. This was
about 80 million years ago.

Chapter 2

Deadly Claws

Velociraptor had a long claw on each foot. The claw was on its second toe. The claw was held off the ground.

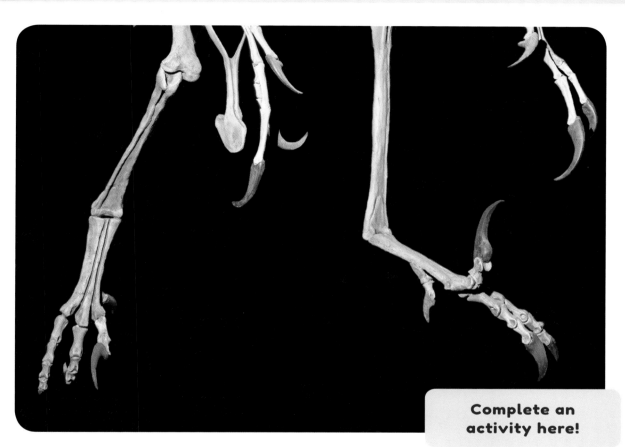

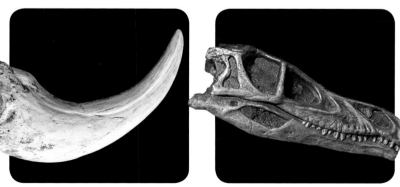

Complete an activity here!

Many scientists think Velociraptor used these claws to hunt. It could slash and grab its **prey**.

Some scientists think the claws had another use. They could be used to climb trees.

The dinosaur also had a strong tail. The tail helped it balance while it attacked. The dinosaur could stand on one foot. It could attack with its other foot. It could balance with its tail.

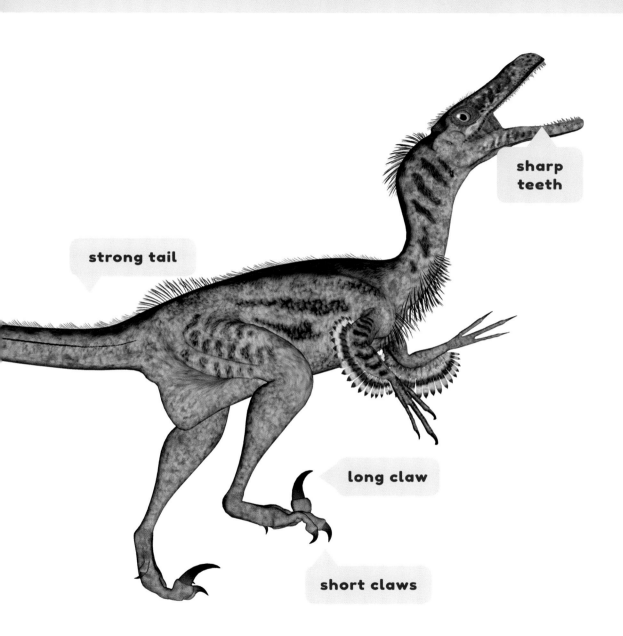

Chapter 3

Feathered Dinosaurs

People once thought Velociraptors were scaly like lizards. But today scientists believe Velociraptors had feathers.

an old idea of what Velociraptor looked like

Learn more here!

Velociraptor's arm bones have small bumps. Birds today have similar bumps. These bumps are where feathers attach to the bones.

Velociraptor's arms were too small for flight.

Chapter 4

A Famous Fossil

A **fossil** was found in Mongolia in 1971. It shows two dinosaurs fighting. One is a Velociraptor. The other is a Protoceratops. This is a plant-eating dinosaur.

Scientists think sand buried the dinosaurs suddenly. It froze them in a fighting pose. The fossil has become famous.

Making Connections

Text-to-Self

What would you do if you met a Velociraptor in real life?

Text-to-Text

Have you read any other books about dinosaur predators? What did you learn?

Text-to-World

Scientists believe Velociraptor had feathers. What animals today have feathers? How do they hunt?

Glossary

Cretaceous Period – a period that lasted from about 145 million years ago to 66 million years ago.

fossil – the remains of a plant or an animal from a long time ago.

predator – an animal that hunts other animals.

prey – an animal that is hunted by other animals.

Index

Online Resources

popbooksonline.com

Thanks for reading this Cody Koala book!

Scan this code* and others like it in this book, or visit the website below to make this book pop!

popbooksonline.com/velociraptor

*Scanning QR codes requires a web-enabled smart device with a QR code reader app and a camera.